Hacker & Virus Protection – The Complete Guide

Nitin Jain

4. Erasing Digital Footprints 45

Information your browser hoards 45

Incognito mode 52

Private and secure web browsing 54

Clearing Your Windows most recently used (MRU) Records 55

The Windows Registry 56

Wiping your registry 57

Improving your system boot time 62

5. File Security 67

Keeping your computer data secured 67

BitLocker 69

How to set up BitLocker 70

TPM 71

6. Secure File Removal 76

The science of file removal 76

Virtually Shredding Your Data 79

Selling or giving away an old computer? 84

7: Computer forensics (Advanced Users) 86

Computer autopsy 86

ACKNOWLEDGMENTS

This book would not be possible without the help of my colleagues, friends and my family. Thanks to all the security developers and experts who have been quoted in this book.

DEDICATION

I dedicate this book to my friends and family who helped me
in drafting the content.

Contents

Introduction 1

1.   **Computer System – Maximum Security** 2

The Binary Internals of Antivirus Software 3

What does antivirus software do?...4

Sanctioned antivirus software 4

Two heads are better than one 7

Paid Anti Virus and AntiSpyware Softwares 9

Securing your Web Browser 12

Slap spoofers and phishers in the face 14

2. **Hermetic Surveillance** 22

Computer ports..22

Protecting your computer ports 24

Implementing Firewalls...26

Firewall Solutions..26

Application Firewall 29

3. **Protecting Wireless Networks & Hotspots** 30

The Pearls of Wireless Networks and Hotspots...........................30

Network enhancements 33

File and printing sharing 35

Public folder sharing 35

Router protection system 37

Change the default settings 38

Keep Your Service Set Identifier (SSID) Number Broadcasting On............39

Common security threat available in Windows 43

Introduction

The internet can be a scary place. Cybersecurity and hacking is not just something for the big corporations or Governments to worry about; it can affect you too.

There are plenty of criminals (termed as 'Hackers') using the Worldwide Web every second trying to infect your machine, steal your credit card information, and hijack your personal or business email and social network accounts.

This is just the beginning. I can point you to several scary real stories in which everyday web users lives have changed from security threats that they never saw coming.

The primary goal of this book is to prevent this from happening to YOU.

If you are browsing the web without any security mechanisms in place, you are exposing your computer and your data to unauthorized access.

Don't fear cybercriminals, but beware of the dangers that they are capable of doing and protect yourself as best as possible with these methods.

Let's get to it!

1. Computer System – Maximum Security

The very first thing I want to accomplish is to bring you up to speed with the primary computer security methods.

I would recommend installing what I coin the **'aegis security package'** at a bare minimum. Below are the details of it:

- Antivirus software
- Anti-spyware software
- Secured browser
- Backup tools
- Firewall

The good news is tons of companies will provide you with these software applications for one hundred percent free! You may be wondering why so generous? Good question! These companies tend to offer some software for free but offer other commercial solutions such as additional software or support.

Anyhow, the very first software that I would recommend installing is antivirus software. But before I get to which products I recommend lets first understand how antivirus software works.

The Binary Internals of Antivirus Software

An anti-virus (AV) software is a program that detects and removes malware from your computer. The terminology "malware" is very general these days and can comprise of:

- Computer viruses
- Trojan horses
- Rootkits
- Worms
- Adware
- Spyware
- Keyloggers

What does antivirus software do?

There are several ways that antivirus software can remove viruses from your computer, but one of the most common is to use heuristics to search for suspicious patterns in executable files. If the AV software spots a program that looks leery, then it will either quarantine it or remove it from your computer.

Quarantine is when a suspected malware program is removed from it's installed location and placed into a location on your computer in which it cannot negatively affect it. The reason why some AV software has this feature is so that researchers can study it and find ways to combat it. The program must still be on your computer for the anti-virus company to research it.

Sanctioned antivirus software

From my research, the best free antivirus program is Avast Free Antivirus. You can download it here: https://www.avast.com

Here is my quick review of Avast.

Installation: This process takes roughly three minutes which is within the average download time of AV software.

I tend to like my programs to be small and compact so that it doesn't slow down my computer, but I'm willing to use a heavier program if it's effective in what it does, and Avast is.

The download size if roughly 70 MB which is around the average size of standard AV software. After you install the software, you do not need to restart your computer like you do many other software programs so you can use it right away.

Interface: The graphical user interface (GUI) of the software is clean and elegant.

There is just enough graphics so that you can see how to easily utilize the tool without it processing slowly. It has tabular buttons on the left portions of the panel so that you can "scan your computer" or utilize any of the other services in the software.

Features: Avast has over 150 million users, and by looking at the security features it's easy to see why. One, it does automatic updates whenever you are connected to the internet.

This is indubitably important because what happens when there is new malware on the internet that the current version of Avast doesn't have any protection for?

Have you ever heard of Zero-day virus? What happens is reliable AV companies like Avast develop heuristics for their software to cope with these new security threats.Once they release these updates called patches your AV program will automatically get the new code once you connect to the web.

Also, Avast is the first free AV software to utilize a file reputation system to evaluate the integrity of downloads. This feature was previously available only in commercial applications like Norton. However, since Avast has a vast community, they are able to leverage off the sheer numbers as users are able to report downloads that they find malicious.

Last but certainly not least, Avast comes with a plugin that helps secure your browser. It does this by spotting fake digital certificates and deterring you from accessing URLs that contain these.

If you are still unsure about using Avast, then feel free to conduct your own research and benchmarks on related AV software. Second, to Avast, I would recommend a less feature extensive ClamWin: http://www.clamwin.com/.

The next part of the Aegis security package is to install spyware software.

Two heads are better than one

The top spyware software applications I would recommend installing are spyware search and destroy or super antispyware free edition. You can download here: http://www.safer-networking.org/dl/.

Keep in mind that spyware software alone is not enough as they should complement antivirus software programs. What I like about Spybot is that it's easy to use, lightweight, backups your registry, and targets malicious adware and code. What I love about super antispyware is that it has an easy to use interface as shown in the screenshot below:

It also has several different scanning options. You can choose from quick, complete, critical, or custom. If you are a newbie, then you can get your feet wet by using the quick scan.

The significant difference between this and the commercial program is the paid one provides real-time protection, or in other words, it adds an extra layer of security to your computing system. The choice to switch to commercial is ultimately up to you, but if you are considering it, then I would recommend trying the 14-day trial first.

Last but not least, if you're wondering what spyware software I would recommend, then I'll give you an answer. I give the edge to SUPERAntiSpyware as from my research its better at detecting and removing spyware from your computer.

Paid Anti Virus and AntiSpyware Softwares

Most of us would, however, would prefer a paid security software that provides advanced features, real-time protection, and other updated features to keep the computer protected from new threats, namely Ransomware.

Over the years, I have used many popular anti-virus software including Kaspersky, Norton, IOBit and many others. However, the following two are my de-facto choices now due to various reasons.

1. Malware Antibytes Premium – cost approx. $50 per machine
2. Quick Heal Total Security – cost approx. $30 per user

Please note I am neither an employee nor an affiliate for any of this paid software.

Malware Antibytes Premium

Awesome!
You're protected.

Malware Antibytes offers a good spectrum of protection, both in terms of virus and ransomware and internet browsing. It does have a high flag rate, meaning it will stop Keygens, pirated software websites or other files that might seem harmless but all in all, it's an excellent solution for virus protection.

The best feature of Malware Antibytes is its ability to protect your system from Ransomware. Head over to Advanced Settings and check all the boxes to get that extra layer of protection.

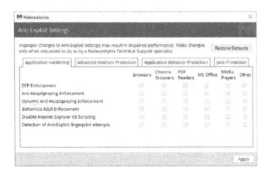

Quick Heal Anti Virus

Quick Heal is not a very popular software outside India; its detection rate is pretty impressive. The scanner is slow, and the first-time install is slow, but it's worth everything. Once installed, Quick Heal runs a very comprehensive scan of your computer which will take very long. But once it's done, the software gives your system reliable protection against anything that might skip Malwarebytes. And many things do skip Malwarebytes which Quick Heal addresses.

Like I mentioned before, I am not an affiliate to any of this software anti-virus, so the recommendation is based totally on my experience and observation.

Securing your Web Browser

Your web browser is an extremely crucial focal point in your online security. With your web browser, you can access your email, bank, web hosting, university, and work accounts. When you are using your browser, it's vital that you know you're swimming in water with sharks so it's crucial that you're using the most secured browser that you possibly can.

From my extensive research, **Google Chrome** should be your go-to browser.

The reason that Google Chrome is very reliable due to the anti-exploit sandbox technology built into it, which partitions the browser from the rest of the operating system. This is ideal because let's say that in the worst case scenario your browser gets malicious code injected into it, the malicious program will not be able to penetrate other parts of your computer because of this security feature.

However, just because Google Chrome is the most secured browser doesn't mean that it is immune to getting hacked because that is just not the case!

Hackers are always looking for ways around security so you should think of security as adding multiple layers.

Never think that you are 100% safe just because you have a program or two installed.

Always stay up to date with the latest security vulnerabilities online. You can do this by following the blogs of malware prevention companies.

With that being said, installing Google Chrome as your primary browser is one step in the right direction. You can download Google Chrome here: https://www.google.com/intl/en/chrome/browser/

Slap spoofers and phishers in the face

The most important step you can take in securing your emails and your browser activity is to make sure that you are using a secured connection.

How do you know that the PayPal invoice that your freelancer sent you isn't a spoof site? For all, you know it could be a spurious site they created to extort your PayPal login credentials. You click on the order link, enter in your PayPal info, and then they have access to your PayPal account. Even if PayPal freezes your account because someone accessed it from a different IP address, all of your hard earned money will be gridlocked on the internet, and you may never see it again!

So, how do you fix this issue? Luckily, the solution is quite simple and also quite sophisticated. All you need to do is carefully look at the URL in the browser. One, is it using a derivative of the authentic URL? For example, does it say **paypa1.com**?

At first glance, you may seem no harm in clicking on this as it looks like the real thing, but be warned that it's not! The very last character in the domain name is the number "1" as opposed to the letter "l."

So, to confirm that you are signing on to the real URL make sure to look for the https at the beginning of the URL as highlighted in the screenshot below:

If a hacker manages to sniff your data with hacking software, the data will be incomprehensible to them once they get it.

There is a Google Chrome extension that will automatically use https on many websites you visit. You can install this extension by going here: https://chrome.google.com/webstore/detail/https-everywhere/gcbommkclmclpchllfjekcdonpmejbdp?hl=en

To install this extension, click on the "Add to Chrome" button highlighted in the screenshot below:

Upon doing so, you will be directed to a pop-up box as indicated in the screenshot below:

15

If you feel comfortable with having your data being accessed by the application, then click the "Add" button.

If not, then click Cancel. Keep in mind that this message shows up with ALL Chrome extensions. Also, bear in mind that you can always uninstall extensions that you no longer need.

You can uninstall extension by:

1. Clicking the Chrome menu

2. Clicking on tools

3. Selecting extensions

4. Clicking the trashcan icon

Anyhow, there are several additional extensions that I would recommend installing on Chrome so that you can maximize your internet security.

Adblock

No security book can be complete without mentioning Adblock. It's one of the most useful Chrome extensions that save you tons of time, especially on Youtube.

Want to browse the web without those annoying ads?

Adblock serves several purposes in your everyday computing.

- One, you won't have to be annoyed with ads that you have little interest in.
- Two, you won't risk getting your browser injected with malicious code that could come with ads also known as adware.
- Three, your computer performance should speed up.

To download Adblock click here:
http://adblockplus.org/en/chrome

Adblock doesn't block all ads; you can read up by their guidelines. If you want to block all ads, then you can do this by modifying the extension's settings in Chrome.

Ghostery

Did you know that some websites track your browsing information? They do this with the help of third-party page elements called trackers. Trackers are used by big sites like Facebook because they are providing their product for free, and when they do this, it's usually at your privacy. The good news is there is an extension that can help circumvent this issue called Ghostery.

You can install it here:
https://chrome.google.com/webstore/detail/ghostery-%E2%80%93-privacy-ad-blo/mlomiejdfkolichcflejclcbmpeaniij?hl=en

WOT

Do you think some links you click on could go to lewd sites you can't trust? I mean, you never know what a link that someone posts on a blog or forum could take you these days so it would be good if there were some type of extension that has an accurate database of websites you can trust.

Well, the closest thing you can get to this is called WOT, and here is the homepage: https://chrome.google.com/webstore/detail/wot-web-of-trust-website/bhmmomiinigofkjcapegjjndpbikblnp?hl=en

How this plugin works is users can rank the trustfulness of the websites that they visit. This is great because if

one million web users are saying that a particular website is full of sneaky malware injections, then it's probably a good idea to avoid it!

Cobian Backup

When good guys think of one solution, bad guys are trying to find loopholes around it. It's vital that you read and implement the methods in this info product, but who knows, a friend or family member could use your computer and inadvertently get malware on it, you just never know.

What I would recommend is to continually backup your information. If you have the latest version of files on your computer, then you will survive any issues that your computer could undergo. Yes, you can try and retrieve the data once your computer is infected, but that becomes magnitudes more difficult, so why put that pressure on yourself?

So, with that being said I would recommend Cobian backup. Cobian Backup (up to version 11, Gravity) has an easy to use interface and is also a very lightweight program. You can also schedule your backups which is an added plus. You can download the application here: https://www.cobiansoft.com/cobianbackup.html

Comodo Backup

Comodo Backup is also a good option for taking a backup of your data. From backing up data and files, offering online storage, self-recovery to scheduling, you can expect all the primary backup and restoration option from this software. As a primary function, it helps users to back-up their online data by protecting the files and allowing them to access it from any system. Comodo offers free 10GB of online storage for backups.

Well, that concludes the Aegis security package. Wait, no it doesn't! There is one more essential element of the Aegis package which is adding a Firewall.

However, since this topic is very in depth, I decided to save it for the next chapter. Continue at your own time and convenience.

2. Hermetic Surveillance

Computer ports

Computer ports identify the different processes are running on a computer and then allow them to share a single physical connection.

A good analogy of computer ports is to compare it to television. Think of a computer as a TV and the ports as the channels. You can tune into hundreds of different channels on the television. There are currently 65,536 different computer ports available!

Several of these ports are reserved for specific types of internet traffic like emails, web surfing, and live chats which are the first 1024 ports (0-1023 as computer numbering always start at 0). The most well-known ports are:

- 20 & 21: File transfer protocol (FTP)
- 22: Secure Shell (SSH)
- 43: Whois
- 80: Hypertext transfer protocol
- 194: IRC chat
- 443: HTTPS secure, encrypted websites via SSL

Besides the first 1024 ports, all the remaining ports have not been given a specific purpose and are open to other uses such as file storage. What you should make a note of is that the higher range ports (49152-65535) are considered private, and are notorious for setting off red flags in your firewall software for being malicious programs.

If you are curious to see what ports are open on your windows operating system then enter in the command netstat —a in the search button on your Windows operated machine as indicated in the screenshot below:

Upon doing so you should get a terminal window that looks something like the screenshot below:

If you're new to using the command line in Windows then you should initially have no idea what all this means so I will try and demystify this for you.

Protocol	Local Address	Foreign Address	State
Either TCP or UDP. The main difference between these two is TCP is a two-way communication channel while UDP is one way. UDP is also quicker, hence is why online game networks tend to use this protocol. Examples of protocols that use TCP are HTTP, HTTPS, FTP, and Telnet.	Your local machine name or its IP on the port.	The remote machine name on the port, or in other words the other machine that your computer is communicating with.	Its either established (transmitting data) or waiting (connection made but no data is being transferred).

If you see any ports that look suspicious then immediately close the program that's running it, as a port can't be running if the process that created it is closed.

Protecting your computer ports

It's a good idea to test your ports so that you can help secure them from hackers. The best way to do this is to emulate a hacker and see which ports you have opened and close the unnecessary ones.

One tool that will help you accomplish this is Steve

Gibson's port analyzer:

https://www.grc.com/x/ne.dll?bh0bkyd2

First, click on the Proceed button, and then select all service ports.

The web application will analyze the status of your system's first 1056 ports. Hopefully, you should see a nice little green grid as indicated below.

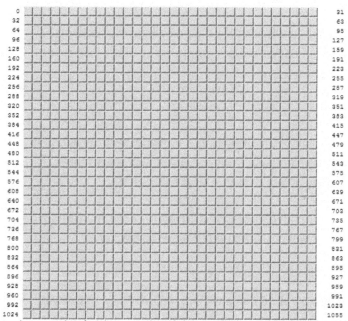

This means that your system has passed the tests and your system data isn't available to the entire internet!

Implementing Firewalls

Implementing a firewall is the last portion of the Aegis security package, and it is one of the most important programs you can have for security purposes.

Firewalls analyze traffic data also known as packets before it comes to your computer to make sure that it is NOT malware.

Just think of the firewall as a personal security agent. It virtually stands by your computer and checks the identity of any data that tries to reach it.

If the identity looks suspicious or is in fact malware, then it will get kicked out of your computer.

Firewall Solutions

Window 7 & 10 come with their own Firewall software, but there are alternative solutions on the market that you may want to consider.

However, before you install any third party application, I would recommend disabling your Windows Firewall as it's not a good idea to have two Firewalls running synchronously.

To do this select start-> control panel->system and security->windows firewall.

Once there you can select the "Turn Windows Firewall on and off" link as indicated in the screenshot below:

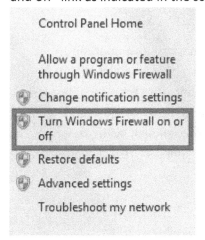

Comodo Firewall

Comodo is an internet protection suite developed by the Comodo group. It also comes with antivirus software, but you can download just the firewall if you already downloaded Avast. The reason why I recommend Comodo is because it consistently has a high score in their protection level. There is a group that tests and measures firewall security known as the Matousec Transparent Security, and they have consistently included Comodo in

27

the top three firewall programs.

Also, the Comodo Firewall program has been labeled top choice by PC Magazine and Gizmo Tech Support. If you have no idea if you should disable Windows Firewall program and use Comodo, then I would give you some sage advice.

Windows is currently the most popular operating system which makes it a prime target by hackers. It is also not uncommon for Windows to have security vulnerabilities and undergo security patches to fix these issues. This right here is enough evidence for me to disable my current Windows Firewall and use a more robust solution.

You can download the freeware for Comodo here: http://personalfirewall.comodo.com/free-download.html

Zone Alarm:

ZA is another freeware program that you can use. The main difference between this and Comodo is that this is more simple and user-friendly. To download the free version of Zone alarm go here: https://www.zonealarm.com/software/free-firewall/

Application Firewall

An application firewall is a type of firewall which controls the input and output of system calls via an application. It does this by monitoring the system and stopping input, output, and calls that don't conform to the system's standards.

One firewall application that I would recommend using is PeerBlock: http://www.peerblock.com/releases.

Peerblock keeps a database of malicious IPs and periodically updates them.

These IPs are not allowed to access your computer or less for one reason or the other you configure the app so they do so within the parameters of the software.

3. Protecting Wireless Networks & Hotspots

The Pearls of Wireless Networks and Hotspots

Wireless networking has come a long way since its beginning stages. You can benefit from it while you're in your local cybercafé sipping on mocha and working on your latest project.

However, you should know that wireless networks tend to contain many threats and are a prime target by hackers. One standard method that malicious users engage in is known as wardriving, which is the process of picking up wifis in an area while in a motor vehicle.

A computer is used to dial various phone numbers in the hope of finding a modem. This is something you cannot stop or less you are a network administrator.

However, it's essential that you keep your computer secured so that if the hacker gets into the network they won't be able to compromise your machine for their devilment.

Besides understanding basic computer security, you should understand the basic hardware components in your computer.

For example, every computer these days come with a wifi card which you should know about.

The reason for this is some of these cards may have security vulnerabilities in them which could be exploited by hackers!

So, find the wifi card your computer is using and Google it to see if you can find any online communities in which individuals are discussing it. If you're using a Windows, you can find what wifi card in your Device Manager.

Click on Network adapters as indicated in the screenshot below:

After doing so, you should be able to find out what network card your computer is utilizing. Google it and find out what others are saying about it. It's crucial because if hackers could take over your connection, then they can do all sorts of evil like spam, or launch malicious malware from your computer and with your IP address!

Network enhancements

Believe it or not, previous versions of the Windows operating system came with file sharing on which allowed hackers to set up backdoor malicious programs. The good news is that Windows 7 AND 10 came with this feature disabled, but there are still some other options that I would recommend modifying.

In the Window's start menu type in "advanced sharing settings" as indicated in the screenshot below and press enter.

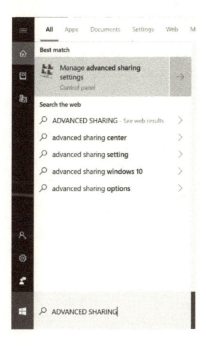

A dialog box should promptly appear shown in the screenshot below.

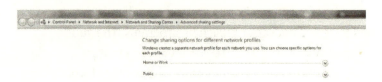

As you can see there are two options that you can select which is "Home or Work," or "Public." "Home or Work" is the settings that you can configure when you are at home browsing the web. Go ahead and click on this option and you should see the following:

Home or Work

Network discovery

When network discovery is on, this computer can see other network computers and devices and is visible to other network computers. What is network discovery?

  ○ Turn on network discovery
  ○ Turn off network discovery

File and printer sharing

When file and printer sharing is on, files and printers that you have shared from this computer can be accessed by people on the network.

  ○ Turn on file and printer sharing
  ○ Turn off file and printer sharing

Public folder sharing

When Public folder sharing is on, people on the network, including homegroup members, can access files in the Public folders. What are the Public folders?

  ○ Turn on sharing so anyone with network access can read and write files in the Public folders
  ○ Turn off Public folder sharing (people logged on to this computer can still access these folders)

Network Discovery

Do you plan on sharing files and printing resources with other computers on the network? If so then you can keep this option on, if not then I would highly recommend disabling this ASAP.

This will add an additional layer of security because you will not be able to see the other computers on the network and conversely they will not be able to see you.

This is good if you have a disgruntled neighbor that wants to hack into your computer from the network and impersonate as you.

File and printing sharing

If you have a family and everyone shares the same networked printer then keep this option on. However, if you plan on being the only person to use the printer then disable this option.

Public folder sharing

There are folders on your Windows 7 AND Windows 10 powered machine that is denoted as public, and they are shown in the screenshot below.

Libraries
    Documents
   ♪ Music
   🖼 Pictures
   🎞 Videos

The files shared in these folders can be shared with others on the network. This could be useful if you have a family and want to easily share files or images without sending each other emails and populating your already thronged email accounts. However, if this does not apply to you, then I would highly recommend disabling this option.

Once all of your settings have been configured click on the "Save settings" option to have your changes propagate. Enjoy the extra satisfaction of security!

Router protection system

If you have high-speed internet access, you more than likely have a router, a router is a box-like an object that has blinking green lights all over it.

What it does is it forwards packets to its ultimate destination. Wireless routers are extremely popular these days and for a good reason. Who wants to manage a bunch of messy wires that gets disordered easily and is difficult to keep neat?

I know I don't, and I think many computing consumers wholeheartedly agree with me. However, due to its popularity and how much control they can gain once they hijack it, hackers are always looking for routers to crack.

Let's take some proper precautions to secure them.

Change the default settings

This seems like common sense, but believe it, or not common sense is not all that common these days. You need to change BOTH the default username and password for your router if you want to increase the security of your network.

Don't use the name of your pet, or anything that can be easily pinned to you if you don't want outsiders knowing which network you are on. Make sure that both the username and password are random and obscure.

Also, your password should contain at least one uppercase letter, a number, and a special character. Default Usernames and passwords are all too easy to find these days.

Keep Your Service Set Identifier (SSID) Number
Broadcasting On

You have probably read from other sources that turning off your SSID will help protect your network from malicious intruders.

However, I would like to tell you that this is the optimum of false security. The only thing this will do is stop a complete and utter newbie from coming on your network, but it does squat to prevent a determined and experienced hacker from gaining access to your SSID.

There are several methods hackers can use to discover your SSID, and one such method (out of five) is to get it via

39

beacon frames. These are little packets of data that are broadcasted periodically to make the presence of a local area network (LAN) known to any network interface cards (NICs).

Beacon frames contain all of the information of a network including the SSID. Hackers have sophisticated tools in which they can sniff this data. Also, cloaking your network name could prove to be an issue for customers. Let's say you own a café at an air shuttle called "Hyena Joe's Coffee Shop," and you have cloaked the network because you don't want any passengers to access your network while waiting for their flight.

This may seem like a good idea on paper, but a devious hacker may come and setup a fake network name called "John's Cafe Free Super-Fast Wireless" that is actually a trap for anyone that connects to it.

A customer from John's Cafe may log onto the network and have all of their browsing data stolen from the hacker including their email and Facebook login credentials.

The two most critical things

The first step to a secured router is making sure you're using the strongest encryption mechanism possible. WEP is puny, it's been beaten and bloodied to a pulp by hackers and it's so easy to crack these days that even a beginner script kiddy could do it.

Next in line is WPA encryption which was created by the Wi-Fi Alliance. This is an upgrade from the previous WEP encryption mechanism.

However, bear in mind that this will only work on WPA protocols that implement the Temporal Key Integrity Protocol (TKIP) algorithm, and will not work on devices that use AES for encryption.

So, let's move along the line. The current best wireless encryption mechanism is known as WPA3 which is also developed by the Wi-Fi Alliance.

WPA3™ is the next generation of Wi-Fi security and provides cutting-edge security protocols to the market. Building on the widespread success and adoption of Wi-Fi CERTIFIED WPA2™, WPA3 adds new features to simplify Wi-Fi security, enable more robust authentication, deliver increased cryptographic strength for highly sensitive data markets, and maintain resiliency of mission-critical networks.

All WPA3 networks:

- Use the latest security methods
- Disallow outdated legacy protocols
- Require the use of Protected Management Frames (PMF)

Since Wi-Fi networks differ in usage purpose and security needs, WPA3 includes additional capabilities specifically for personal and enterprise networks. Users of WPA3-Personal receive increased protections from password guessing attempts, while WPA3-Enterprise users can now take advantage of higher grade security protocols for sensitive data networks.

WPA3, which retains interoperability with WPA2™ devices, is currently an optional certification for Wi-Fi CERTIFIED devices. It will become required over time as market adoption grows. (Source: https://www.wi-fi.org/discover-wi-fi/security)

Well, it's more like a defect in the hardware. Stay far away from routers that come with Wi-Fi Protected Setup (WPS) as this is where the vulnerability lies. The idea of WPS is not entirely bad as its primary goal is to make it easy for non-technical folks to set up their wifi.

However, with the pros come cons. The con far outweighs the advantages because a hacker can easily use a brute force attack to get the WPS pin, and then all bets are off.

It is suggested to turn off the WPS feature, but this is physically no feasible in all router models because WPS is hardwired into it. My recommendation is if you're using a router that has WPS then get rid of it ASAP and get a router that uses WPA3 and doesn't have the WPS feature.

Common security threat available in Windows

Hackers are always actively searching for the administrator account to break into. The reason for this is because the admin has unlimited power.

They can create new accounts, install software, change settings, and view the files on all the other accounts stored on a computer. So, the method that I would highly encourage for you to use that will increase your security is to change the admin username which is super easy to do.

Go to 'User Accounts' and Family Safety->User accounts.

Select your current administrator account and then change the username, and then it's done that easily!

In addition, I would highly recommend setting up a dummy admin account so that it can be a trap for hackers.

The reason why this is a must because if a hacker realizes that you have renamed your admin account to something other than "admin", then they will proceed to search your system for the correct username.

However, if you set up a dummy admin account which is just a regular account with limited privileges but named "admin," then you can outsmart the hacker!

In the worst case scenario even if they do infiltrate your system, they won't be able to have full power as they will just be a user with limited privileges.

4. Erasing Digital Footprints

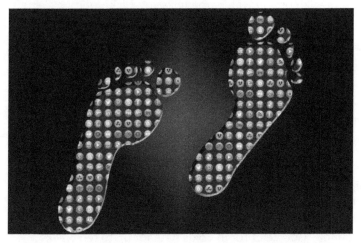

If a hacker is able to discover your browsing habits, then they can compile a virtual profile about you, and will probably know more information about you than your closest friends, family, or significant other! Let's stop them from doing this.

Information your browser hoards

Browsers know a lot more information about you than you think. I would highly recommend reading the privacy policy of the browsers you use.

- Google chrome privacy policy
- Firefox privacy policy
- Internet Explorer privacy policy
- Safari privacy policy

Browsers record every single site you visit, every image you look at, the videos you watch, the links you click, your favorite websites, and the content of your downloads. A good chunk of this information is stored in the browser's cache, history, and cookies.

If you have people coming over your house, and if you let them use your computer without deleting your history, then they will be able to discover all the websites that you visit in a "variable" amount of days. The reason why I said a variable is because depending on the browser you're using it will hold the data for a different amount of time.

For example, Google Chrome holds data for up to ten weeks while in default mode. Also, browsers store HTTP cookies, colloquially known as "cookies" which are small text files stored on your computer to help identify you.

Virtually all shopping carts use these such as Amazon, Godaddy, and eBay. Cookies are stored in the browser when you visit a site, and they can be retrieved once you return. This allows the site to remember your settings, what products you looked at, and various activities that you took on the website.

Depending on the default settings on your browser the average web user has no idea that cookies are stored on their computer, and some websites use several cookies. Cookies may seem harmless at first glance because they help you to personalize the sites you visit, but it also has several drawbacks.

One, the cookie identifies you by your IP address, and this is a way for the site you're using to build a highly detailed account of you. They can then sell this highly detailed data to third-party advertisers that you have no idea what their intentions are. Also, just by having a cookie on your site is privacy vulnerability as it will reveal the websites you visited as indicated in the screenshot below:

No worries, I'll show you how to delete all the history and cookies on your site. However, if you want you can disable cookies from entering your computer in the first place.

Here are the instructions on how to do this in Chrome:

1. Click on the Chrome menu button.

2. Select the settings option as highlighted in the screenshot below:

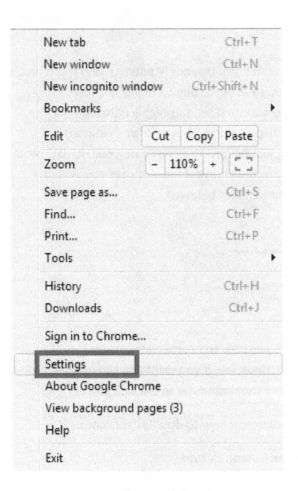

New tab	Ctrl+T
New window	Ctrl+N
New incognito window	Ctrl+Shift+N
Bookmarks	▶
Edit	Cut	Copy	Paste
Zoom	−	110%	+	⛶
Save page as...	Ctrl+S
Find...	Ctrl+F
Print...	Ctrl+P
Tools	▶
History	Ctrl+H
Downloads	Ctrl+J
Sign in to Chrome...
Settings
About Google Chrome
View background pages (3)
Help
Exit

3. Select "Show advanced settings" as highlighted below.

Default browser

Make Google Chrome my default browser

Google Chrome is not currently your default browser.

Show advanced settings...

4. Click on the "Content settings..." button as indicated in the screenshot below. 4. Click on the "Content settings..." button as indicated in the screenshot below.

Privacy

Content settings... | Clear browsing data...

Google Chrome may use web services to improve your browsing experience. You may optionally disable these services. Learn more

☑ Use a web service to help resolve navigation errors

☑ Use a prediction service to help complete searches and URLs typed in the address bar

☑ Predict network actions to improve page load performance

5. Select "Block third-party cookies and site data" as indicated in the screenshot below.

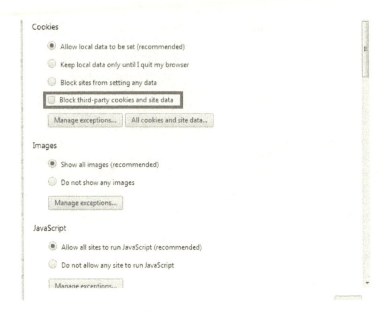

Also, you can disable JavaScript as some jackass coders try to inject malicious code into your browser by using JavaScript.

Keep in mind though by disabling JavaScript you may miss out on some interactive features used with web pages.

Let's switch gears and worry about deleting all your previous browsing information. The good news is its straightforward to remove your past history, cookies, and cache from web browsers.

Below are the steps to deleting your browser history with Chrome.

1. Click on the Chrome menu buttons indicated in the screenshot below.

2. Click on Tools, and then click on "Clear browsing data" as highlighted in red in the screenshot below.

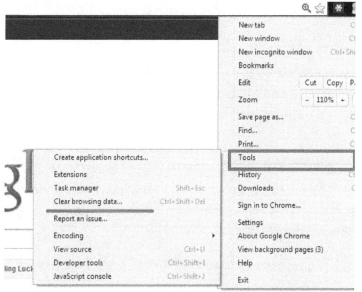

3. Select "Clear browsing data" as highlighted in the screenshot below.

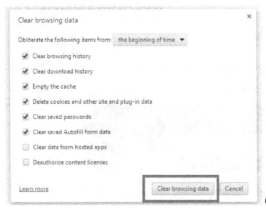

Congratulations, you have deleted your browsing data, cookies, cache, passwords, and auto-fill information that was automatically saved in Google Chrome.

Incognito mode

Most web browsers have an option in which you can browse the web without having your history saved, and Google's Chrome version of this is called "Incognito."

Note, all this means is that your current web history will not be saved, but this does NOT mean that any activity you do can't be traced back to you. Just bear in mind that wherever you navigate to online, you leave a digital footprint in the form of your IP address.

Following are the steps you can take to enter stealth mode in Google Chrome.

1. Click on the Chrome menu button.

2. Click on the "New incognito window" tab as indicated in the screenshot below.

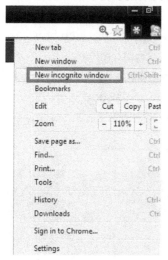

3. Browse the web without having your history stored in your browser. You should see an icon figure with a gray hat and suit in the upper left hand corner of the screen.

Now you can browse the web without having your surfing history saved.

Private and secure web browsing

Epic Privacy Browser

I love the Epic Browser! It's private and secure web browser blocks ads, trackers, fingerprinting, crypto mining, ultrasound signaling and more. Stop 600+ tracking attempts in an average browsing session. You can also turn on network privacy with their free VPN (servers in 8 countries).

Download it from here - https://www.epicbrowser.com/

Clearing Your Windows most recently used (MRU) Records

Windows operated machines store your most recently used files on your computer. This means that even if you deleted your browsing behavior, many of the files that you accessed recently are still in the archives on your computer. Below are the quick steps that you should take to delete the most recently used files on your computer.

1. Open up the taskbar: To do this enter the text "taskbar" in the Windows search box.

2. Click on "Start Menu", and then under Privacy unselect the store and display options which are highlighted below.

After doing so select "OK" to have the changes propagate.

The Windows Registry

As mentioned previously, Windows store your most recently used applications, but unfortunately, this is just the beginning of a long journey in data removal. Windows keeps a database of information on your computer within registries. Your registry can keep information about the:

- Name and type of files you download
- The source of your downloaded files
- Passwords you have stored in the applications you use
- List of mounted storage devices
- List of wireless networks that the computer connects to

By now you should realize that having this information stored on your computer is probably not a good idea. Some computer forensic software can quickly extract and analyze the data from your registry in a matter of seconds! Let's learn how to clean the registry to avoid your most sensitive information from being exploited.

Keep in mind that the following section is for advanced users as if you accidentally delete a registry that your operating systems need then you will effectively prevent it from booting. Also, if you consider yourself a basic Windows user, then I would recommend skipping forward to this section and have the software execute this process for you.

Wiping your registry

Step One: In the start window, type in the text "regedit" and click enter.

You should see a window appear as indicated in the screenshot below:

Step Two: Use the search option

From there, select Edit->Find to search for files that you may have embedded within the registries. You can repeat the search phrase throughout the entire registries by selecting F3.

Keep iterating throughout the registries until you get a message that states that you have came to the end of it. Keep in mind that the searches are not case sensitive, so "banking info" is not the same as "Banking Info." Some sample files that you can query are:

- Files that contain sensitive information about you. Do you have a health issue, or do you have some personal family images?
- The download path on your machine.

- File extensions associated with your sensitive data. For example, .txt, .mpg, .jpg,.torrent, and .mp3 files.

Once you locate any sensitive data, it's time to remove them. First, add the records that you want to delete to the Registry Editor's Favorites for future reference. To do this, just go to the menu and select Favorites->Add to Favorites. Once that is done you can then utilize this date to clear the registry.

The final step in the deletion process is to double click on the item that your query displayed, remove the value data, and then click OK to save.

Deleting Temporary Files

Most modern day operating systems implement virtual memory, which is a memory management method that "virtualizes" the physical architecture of a computing system.

This allows computer programs to be modeled as if there is only one type of memory, which is virtual. Computer programs that consume large amounts of data like screen recording software will create temporary files to reduce the workload on the machine.

The issue with temporary files is sometimes they stay

on the computer. This most likely happens because the developer forgot to write code that will remove the temporary files once the program is no longer running, which is bad for two main reasons. One, these temp files can leave behind sensitive data that you thought was deleted. If a malicious user gains access to your machine and extracts the contents of your temp files, then they will be able to find out a whole lot of information about you. Secondly, temp files can build up very quickly and consume a lot of memory on your computer which will make your system sluggish.

I'm quite convinced that you don't want this to happen, so I'm going to show you how you can easily remove the TEMP files from your computer. If you are an advanced user and don't want to install additional freeware on your machine, then you can quickly view the temp files on your computer by going to this path on your computer: C:\WINDOWS\TEMP.

From here you can delete the temp files that you no longer need.

Save all the Hassle with CCleaner

Alternatively, you can consider using a quality piece of freeware called CCleaner, which you can download here. Once you open it, you should come to an interface that looks like the screenshot below.

As you can see this software comes with many features. It allows you to clear not only the temporary files but also a lot of data that is left in your Windows operating system.

To clean your computer click "Analyze" which will show you the files, and select the clean button to remove them. Once that is done you should receive a message that the cleaning has been completed and that X amount of bytes have been cleared from your system as indicated in the screenshot below:

```
CLEANING COMPLETE - (128.093 secs)
------------------------------------------------
10,157 MB removed.
------------------------------------------------
```

However, cleaning temp files, history, and cookies is one of the many features that this application offers, so let's explore more! Next, click on the "Applications" tab. You should see an interface that looks like the screenshot below:

This allows you to clean the data that many of the applications you use leave behind. Also, another feature that it comes with is a registry cleaner which you can access by clicking on the "Registry" icon on the left-hand column of the application.

Scan for issues and then fix them. Most of the problems will occur because the program is trying to reference a dynamic-link library (DLL) that no longer exists at the location, and then it will then ask for your permission to delete the registry value which you can select.

Improving your system boot time

In CCleaner click on tools and then select startup, which should take you to the interface in the software application indicated below:

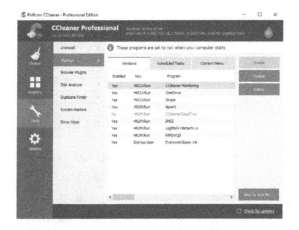

This displays the programs that automatically execute at startup. If your computer is slow during startup, then this is an intelligent way to speed it up. Just select the applications that you do not want to start during the system boot, and then click the "Disable" button. You will still be able to use this application; it just won't automatically run when your machine boots.

Wiping the cached DNS entries

The domain name system (DNS) was created so that we wouldn't have to enter in IP addresses into web browsers! Without DNS we would have to enter something like 64.233.191.255 into our browser to access Google. Imagine entering these in for all the websites you visit on a daily basis!

So, lo and behold, we have DNS that matches a word to a string of numbers so that we won't have to torture ourselves entering in IP addresses into browsers. Every time you visit a site, your operating system see the IP address. However, these IP addresses will remain on your computer even if you use computer cleaning software like CCleaner!

Sophisticated hackers know about this and can retrieve websites that you have been visiting by analyzing the DNS information. To make matters worse, the DNS entries will remain on your site even after you use the stealth feature in your browser like Google incognito.

So let's concentrate on how we can protect our privacy. The first step you should take is prompting the command line in Windows by typing the text "cmd."You should get a terminal window that appears like the screenshot below:

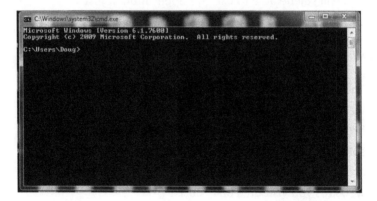

In the terminal type, the text "IPCONFIG/DISPLAYDNS" and then press enter. To copy this text directly into your Windows terminal, you can highlight the text, and then use the keyboard shortcut of ctrl+insert.

Once you go to your terminal, you can right-click in an open space and then select paste, and the text should now be appended there. Below is a snapshot of the contents this query produced:

```
translate.google.com

    Record Name . . . . . : translate.google.com
    Record Type . . . . . : 5
    Time To Live  . . . . : 72
    Data Length . . . . . : 8
    Section . . . . . . . : Answer
    CNAME Record  . . . . : www3.l.google.com

meta.stackoverflow.com

    Record Name . . . . . : meta.stackoverflow.com
    Record Type . . . . . : 1
    Time To Live  . . . . : 80
    Data Length . . . . . : 4
    Section . . . . . . . : Answer
    A (Host) Record . . . : 69.59.197.21

programmers.stackexchange.com

    Record Name . . . . . : programmers.stackexchange.com
    Record Type . . . . . : 1
    Time To Live  . . . . : 147
    Data Length . . . . . : 4
    Section . . . . . . . : Answer
    A (Host) Record . . . : 69.59.197.21

\Users\Doug>
```

As you can see I visited three sites, Google Translate, StackOverflow, and then StackExchange. You may see no harm in this, but there could be several.

What if you visited a health website to research a health issue you have? What if you were going through some financial problems and were doing research about bankruptcy? What if you have an addiction you are trying to stop?

65

Your DNS entries may contain issues that you don't want lingering around on your computer so you are better off nuking it. The solution to this is easy but not as tasty as pie.

Execute the following query in the terminal windows: "IPCONFIG/FLUSHDNS."

Upon doing so, you should get this message that shows in the terminal:

```
C:\Users\Doug>IPCONFIG/FLUSHDNS
Windows IP Configuration
Successfully flushed the DNS Resolver Cache.
C:\Users\Doug>
```

Congratulations, your DNS entries have been erased.

5. File Security

Keeping your computer data secured

If you want to keep your personal computing habits private, then one of the best solutions to this is to use data encryption on the fly. On the fly means that your data will instantly be encrypted before it is saved, and decrypted after it is saved.

This will ensure that your computing activities such as downloading files, viewing videos, and chatting with online friends are done on an **Encrypted Virtual Drive (EVD).**

How EVDs work is it creates a container file on a hard drive that contains a passphrase. Within this container, the data you want to encrypt will be hidden inside and protected by strong encryption.

Once you enter the correct passphrase into the encryption software, it will mount the container file onto your machine. Mounting is the process in which the data files in the virtual drive will become unencrypted, or will be in a format in which you can read.

Without entering the correct passphrase, the data in the virtual drive will be encrypted or illegible to users that view it. For these reasons, I would highly recommend keeping your sensitive files such as your web hosting information, and online account passwords on an encrypted drive.

When you are ready to access the files on the virtual drive, you can dismount or decrypt the information. However, just because you encrypt your data doesn't mean that all of your computing histories will be safeguarded. There are still some security leakages even if you do encrypt your files:

- If you have a web browser that is installed to a non-encrypted location on your machine then all of the data that your browser saved such as the history, cookies, bookmarks, and cache will still be retrievable.

- Most recently used (MRU) data may still be in the registry locations on your unencrypted drives.
- Temporary files may still be left behind.

So remember, keep using the cleaning methods to remove the trace data which was discussed previously. The only way that the encrypted drive will hide these trace data is if you install the virtual drive over your entire operating system which is a little bit trickier to do and is something that should be left to advance users.

BitLocker

The open source software that I would recommend using to create your virtual drives is BitLocker.

BitLocker is Microsoft's easy-to-use, proprietary encryption program for Windows that can encrypt your entire drive, as well as help, protect against unauthorized changes to your system such as firmware-level malware.

You can download the software here - https://www.microsoft.com/en-in/download/details.aspx?id=7806

How to set up BitLocker

Here's how I got BitLocker running on a Windows 8.1 Pro machine. I've also added some Windows 10-specific instructions.

1. Open Windows' Control Panel, type BitLocker into the search box in the upper-right corner, and press Enter.

2. Next, click Manage BitLocker, and on the next screen, click Turn on BitLocker.

3. Now BitLocker will check your PC's configuration to make sure your device supports Microsoft's encryption method.

BitLocker checks for the required Trusted Platform Module.

If you're approved for BitLocker, Windows will show you a message like this one (see screenshot at left). If your TPM module is off, Windows will turn it on automatically for you, and then it will encrypt your drive.

TPM

To activate your TPM security hardware Windows has to shut down completely. Then you'll have to manually restart your PC. Before you do, make sure any flash drives, CDs, or DVDs are ejected from your PC. Then hit Shutdown.

Once you restart your PC, you may see a warning that your system was changed. In my case, I had to hit F10 to confirm the change or press Esc to cancel. After that, your computer should reboot, and once you log in again, you'll see the BitLocker window.

Recovery key and encryption

We've rebooted and the TPM is now active.

After a few minutes, you should see a window with a green check mark next to Turn on the TPM security hardware. We're almost at the point where we'll encrypt the drive! When you're ready, click Next.

71

Before you encrypt your drive, however, you will be asked to enter a password that must be entered every time you turn on your PC, before you even get to the Windows login screen. Windows gives you a choice of either entering the password manually or inserting a USB key. Choose whichever method you prefer, but I recommend sticking with the manual password, so you don't depend on a single USB key for authentication.

Next, you have to save a recovery key just in case you have problems unlocking your PC. Windows gives you three choices for saving this key in Windows 8.1 and Windows 10: Save the file to your Microsoft account, save to a file, save to a flash drive (Windows 10), or print the recovery key. You can choose as many of these options as you'd like, and you should choose at least two.

In my case, I chose to save the file to a USB key and print the key on paper. I decided against saving the file to my Microsoft account because I don't know who has access to the company's servers. That said, saving your key to Microsoft's servers will make it possible to decrypt your files if you ever lose the flash drive or paper containing your recovery key code.

Once you've created two different instances of the recovery key and removed any USB drives, click Next.

Choose whichever option best describes your PC.

On the following screen, you have to decide whether to encrypt only the disk space used so far or encrypt your PC's entire drive. If you're encrypting a brand-new PC without any files, then the option to encrypt only the used disk space is best for you, because new files will be encrypted as they're added. If you have an older PC with a few more miles on the hard drive, you should choose to encrypt the entire drive.

Once you've chosen your encryption scheme, click Next. We're almost there.

Windows 10 only

If you're running Windows 10 build 1511 or later, you'll be asked to choose your encryption mode: new or compatible. If you're encrypting your onboard storage drive, then select new.

73

The compatible mode is mostly for removable drives that will be used with older versions of Windows that do not have the "new" encryption mode.

Make sure the box next to Run BitLocker system check is clicked so that Windows will run a system check before encrypting your drive. Once the box is checked, click Continue... and nothing happens.

You have to reboot your PC to start BitLocker's disk encryption manually.

You'll see an alert balloon in the system tray telling you that encryption will begin after you restart the PC. Restart your PC, and you'll be asked to enter your BitLocker password or insert the USB key you created earlier.

After you log in this final time, you should see another system tray alert telling you that the encryption is in progress.

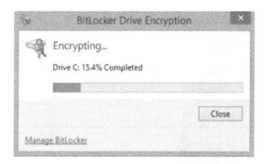

Whew! We made it to the encryption phase.

You can continue to work on your PC during the encryption phase, but things may be running a little more slowly than usual. Consider holding back on anything that might tax your system during initial encryption, such as graphics-intensive programs.

After all those clicks, that's it! Just leave Windows to do its thing, and in a few hours, you'll have a BitLocker-encrypted drive. The length of time it takes BitLocker to fully encrypt your files depends on the size of your drive, or how much data you're encrypting if you're only encrypting existing data on a new PC.

6. Secure File Removal

The science of file removal

Did you know that the files that you delete on your computer can be recovered? Yes, I mean even if you remove them from your recycle bin, or even if you reformat your hard drive it still can be retrieved by computer savvy users! As computing costs goes down, hard drives are now able to hold larger sums of data, which means that your computer is more than likely holding data from several ago through a process called data remanence.

One may be wondering why they should ensure that their data is obliterated. After all, if you're not carrying out illegal operations, then there should be nothing to worry about correct?

Well, even ethical computer users could have data they don't want others to get. For example, you may have web hosting login information in a text file on your computer, or you may have personal family images stored in the Pictures folder. The risks of someone retrieving this data are incredibly high when you decide to sell your old computer or its storage media like USB sticks or external hard drives.

If you do not take the proper precautions to remove your data from these devices, then it can quickly be recovered by hackers and used at their disposal for identity theft!

When you delete a file from the computer your operating system actually doesn't erase it since replacing every byte on a file can take tremendous time and slow the processes of your computer significantly. Since modern day operating systems are quite sophisticated what in fact happens is that an entry to the file is removed, usually the first character so that you will not be able to "see" it or "search" for it on your computer.

However, just because you can't physically see it or search for it doesn't mean that the file does not exist on your computer because the content of it can still be within your machine.

Windows use File Allocation Table (FAT) for its computer file system architecture to store the files on your computer. This is legacy software that is both simple and robust.

Let's say that you have a file called "myjournal.doc" stored on your computer. When this file is deleted from your recycle bin the file is simply modified, and the entry that was previously on the stack is now marked as available so that new data on your computer can be stored in its place.

If many files are added to your computer over time then it is possible that myjournal.doc may actually be erased for good. However, this will depend significantly on the memory limitations of your computer. If it has a lot of memory, then there is a high probability that your deleted data will remain on there.

If you sell your old computer on eBay, Amazon, or at a local garage sale, then all someone needs to do is use a data recovery tool (some are free) to retrieve the old files that are stuck on your hard drive. In summation, when you delete a file from your computer all it tells your OS is that the physical space of where the file was at is now available to be overwritten with fresh data.

Now, let's find out how we can make sure that the files that we delete are forever gone. This will serve numerous benefits such as not worrying about sensitive data being stored on machines that you have given away, and it will also free up extra memory on your computer so that it may run faster.

Virtually Shredding Your Data

Business owners will run their sensitive paper files such as accounting info, medical records, or employee payroll information through paper shredders, and the same process should apply to electronic documents as well. At the bare minimum, you should wipe or securely delete sensitive files and data, and below I will recommend some tools.

CCleaner is an excellent tool for secure file deletion. CCleaner has four methods of secure deletion: a Simple Overwrite (1 pass), DOD 5220.22-M (3 passes), NSA (7 passes), and Gutmann (35 passes). A 'pass' refers to how many times CCleaner writes over the spot on the hard drive. The more times CCleaner writes to that spot, the harder the file will be to recover by any means. The drawback is that it will take CCleaner longer to complete the job.

CCleaner can only securely delete files which have not yet been deleted from the Recycle Bin. If you have already deleted files insecurely (for example, using Windows Explorer), you can remove them securely using Recuva.

Here are some other useful, secure File deletion tools for Windows.

File shredder

This is a quality opensource file deletion program that is compatible with Windows. You can install the application by accessing the download link on the homepage here: http://www.fileshredder.org/.

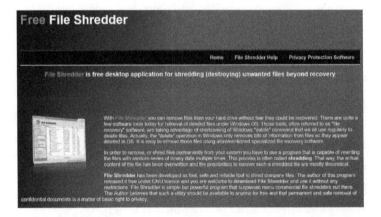

After downloading the application, you should be
taken to an interface that looks like the screenshot
below:

What I like best about this application is that it has a
nice GUI which is good for novices because they will be
able to easily learn how to use the functions of the
software. It also has several simple commands such as
Add File(s) and Add Folder so that you can find the
appropriate files that you wish to destroy and nuke
them easily as indicated in the screenshot below:

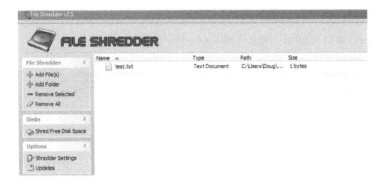

In addition, the program also uses several shredding algorithms with up to 7 passes which means that it will shred the document 7 times.

It's also compliant with the US government DoD 5220-22.M, and the Guttman method. Last but not least, it will also shred free space on your machine. What this means is that the program will overwrite the free space in the memory with random patterns of 0s and 1s so that data recovery will be extremely difficult.

Eraser

This is a security tool for Windows which allows you to securely delete your data. The software accomplishes this by overwriting the data several times with algorithmic patterns. It is licensed under GNU so you can download it freely without paying a fee, and you can also view the source code libraries as well if you are that type of Geek.

You can download the application by going to the download page here:
http://eraser.heidi.ie/download.php

Some of its feature is that it's compatible with the Windows operating systems, easy to use, and works has a customizable Scheduler.

Freeraser

This is another file shredding application, and you can download it by visiting the site here:
http://www.freeraser.com

This is a Windows application that is easy to install and it also uses the DoD 5220.22-M for data sanitization. After you installed the program it places a recycle bin like icon on your Desktop. All you have to do is drag and drop the files that you want to shred into this icon and the program will take care of the rest.

Selling or giving away an old computer?

If you're selling an old computer on eBay or if you want to donate it then I would highly recommend going even one step further. The previous tools makes it possible to wipe files, but the problem is your C drive has tons of files on it that you probably don't want to be recovered like the temp or registry files for example.

You should look for a program that erases all the contents of your hard drive until the data is permanently removed.

The program I recommend for this is Darik's Boot and Nuke, and you can access the homepage here: http://www.dban.org/

As again, only use this program when you are about to get rid of an old computer and do not want any of your data swimming around the hard drive. However, if you are really paranoid then you can take a physical approach to destroying data. You can consider pouring liquid nitrogen over the hard drive and wait for it to freeze. Then you can grab a hammer and thwack it so that it shatters into a thousand little pieces. That seems a little time consuming to me but to each their own.

7: Computer forensics (Advanced Users)

Computer autopsy

In the previous section I discussed methods on how to securely wipe files from your computer. However, if you tend to over think things then you may wonder how can you check to ensure that the files from your computer are gone?

The solution is to use file recovery software and one that I recommend is called Autopsy shown in the screenshot below.

You can visit the homepage here:
http://www.sleuthkit.org/autopsy/

You can download the software here:
http://www.sleuthkit.org/autopsy/download.php

Autopsy is a derivative of software called the "Sleuth Kit", but it is much easier to use because it has a graphical user interface. The Sleuth Kit operates via the command line, and it is much more difficult to operate.

The first step you need to do is create an image of your system files. To do this you should click on the "Create New Case" button on the main screen and then enter the case name and the location that you want to save it to shown in the screenshot below:

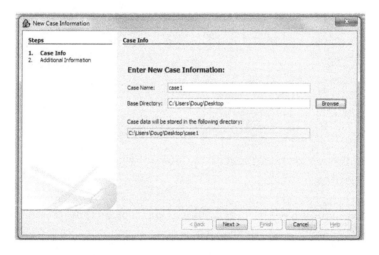

Once that is done, click next (case number is optional). Once that is done the next step is to create a disk image in the "Add Image Wizard."

You will need to supply this with the location of the image that you would like to add. The current image formats that Autopsy supports are E01 and raw dd files.

You can create a system image in Windows 7 by going to Start->Control Panel->System and Security->Backup your computer. Once you are there click on the Backup now button as indicated in the screenshot below:

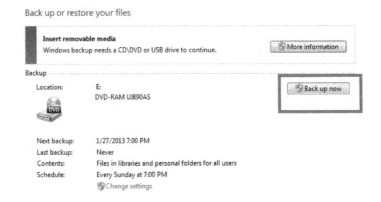

Be prepared to wait several minutes for this process to complete.

If you don't have neither of these then click on the dialog box and select "Local Disk."

After doing the data should load in the main interface as indicated in the screenshot below:

You can navigate through the file structures and look for files that you can recover. If some files were supposed to be deleted but show up here then that is a good indicator that the file wiping program you are using could use another go, or its time to switch to a new software.

In addition you can also consider using "Recuva." This software is from Piriform, the same company that developed CCleaner. Like CCleaner, Recuva is also easy to use.

You can download it by visiting this URL here: http://www.piriform.com/recuva/download

Summary

By now you should know that internet security is a whole lot more complex than installing an antivirus software program. There are so many vulnerabilities out there that it can literally fill an encyclopedia and more.

The good news is if you implement preventive measures and practice the good security habits taught in this product then you will circumvent hackers.

The purpose of security is to not make a system impenetrable as sooner or later hackers will find exploits. The purpose is to add multiple layers of security so that if a hacker does find a loophole then they will have to go through several other security measures in order to break into your system.

Ideally, this circumvention should be so great that hackers will need to spend years cracking your system which will not be worth even their time. Practice safe internet browsing, and stay up to date with the latest security threats. Take care.